1992

OTHER BOOKS BY EAMON GRENNAN

Wildly for Days
What Light There Is & Other Poems
Twelve Poems

Eamon Grennan

AS IF IT
MATTERS

GRAYWOLF PRESS

Publication of this volume is made possible in part by a grant provided by the Minnesota State Arts Board, through an appropriation by the Minnesota State Legislature, and by a grant from the National Endowment for the Arts. Additional support has been provided by the Jerome Foundation, the Northwest Area Foundation, and other generous contributions from foundations, corporations, and individuals. Graywolf Press is a member agency of United Arts, Saint Paul.

As If It Matters was first published by The Gallery Press in 1991 in Ireland where it was edited and designed by Peter Fallon, and typeset by Redsetter Limited of Ireland.

Published by GRAYWOLF PRESS,
2402 University Avenue, Suite 203,
Saint Paul, Minnesota 55114.
All rights reserved.

9 8 7 6 5 4 3 2
First Printing, 1992

Library of Congress Cataloging-in-Publication Data
Grennan, Eamon, 1941-
    As if it matters / Eamon Grennan.
        p.   cm.
    ISBN 1-55597-154-7 : $19.00 : ISBN 1-55597-155-5 (pbk.) : $11.00
    I Title
  PR6067. R398A8'1992
621'.914--DC20   91-29626

Contents

COMPASS READINGS
Two Climbing   *page* 9
Diagnosis   12
Walking Home As the Rain Draws Off   14
Room and Sun   16
Circlings   18
Uphill Home   22
Breaking Points   25
Report from the Front   28
Driving through Fog   29
Family Sketches   30
Kitchen Vision   33
Early Learning   35
Compass Reading   36
Moving   38
Station   41
Walk, Night Falling, Memory of My Father   43

THINGS IN THE FLESH
The Cave Painters   49
Endangered Species   51
Small Mercies   53
Woman at Lit Window   55
Breakfast Room   57
Branchwater   59
Woman Holding a Balance   61
Cows   65
Daughter and Dying Fish   68
Sea Dog   70
Rights   72
One Morning during the Elections   74
Colour Shot   76
That Ocean   78
Leftovers   81
Two Gathering   83

Notes   89
Acknowledgements   91

COMPASS
READINGS

Two Climbing

1

After the blackface sheep, almond coats daubed
to the blush of slaughtered innards,
all I saw going up was a small frog
speckled rust and raw olive, slick
as a lizard, with a lizard's fixed
unblinking eye. It splays and tumbles
to a safe shadow
where heather-roots wind through limestone
while I keep climbing
behind Conor, who's twelve, my heart
starting to knock at thin air, effort. He loves
leading me on, and when I look up
to where he stands waiting — legs apart and
firmly planted on a rock spur, gazing round him
at the mountains and the sea, the thin
ribboning road beige below us, my figure
bent over the flat green hands of bracken —
I'm struck sharp as a heart pain
by the way this minute brims
with the whole story: such touched fullness
and, plain as day, the emptiness at last.

2

Once down again, safe home, we both
look wondering up to the top of Tully Mountain
and the barely visible concrete plinth
that peaks it, on which he sat
exalted for a time and took
the whole of Ireland in, he said,
with one big swivelling glance, and took twelve snaps
to prove it: a windy shimmer of cloud, mountain,
water — a rack of amphibian spirits drifting
over our heads. I saw the way our elevation
simplified the lower world
to rocky crops and patches, neat
green and tea-brown trapezoids
of grass and bog, bright pewtered spheres
of pure reflection. We sat out of the wind
on two flat rocks, and passed
in silence to one another
another sweet dry biscuit
and a naggin whiskey bottle
of water, pleased with ourselves
at some dumb male thing for which
he finds the word: *adventure*. Going down,
he lopes, leads, is deliberately solicitous,
pointing out loose rocks, the treacherous
bright green surface
of a swampy passage, a safer way.
His knowing talk
enlarges airily our trek and conquest.

3

Walking at last the field path
to the house, he is all
straight spine and limber stride
in his mudded wellingtons,
while I note how stone silent
the plum-coloured broad back of the mountain is,
keeping the wind off our lives
in this hollow. Before going in,
he sets on an outside windowsill
the horned sheep skull we salvaged
from the bracken, weathered to a cracked adze
of jawbone ringed and bristling
with broken teeth. Bone-flanged, the great
eye sockets gape, and like fine stitching
the skull's one partition seams dead centre.
In less than a week from now
he'll have forgotten this bony trophy,
but not the journey we took together
to find it — that hammering brisk ascent, the luminous
view of everything, those buffeting winds, unruffled
interlude of quiet, then, in the end,
that sweet leading down. While I'll go on
watching the split skull — colour of crushed almond
or washed-out barley muslin — shine.

Diagnosis

To be touched like that
from so far, collusion
of skin and sunlight — one
ray, one cell, the collapse
of fenceworks: I feel mined,
nicked like a leaf
to a brown spot of burn
that catches the eye. Visited.

With one eye open
I probe the small swelling,
hoping to know
this intimate enemy
that bites through bone
if left to its own
staggering devices: so this —
as if a myth had fallen
into the back garden
and stood in my light
when I took out the trash —
is it. Detached
and absolute, the word
comes over the phone
and day chills a little, ghosted,
goes briefly out of focus.
Somewhere a knife is sharpening;
my skin shivers. I can
see my own skin
as if it were
another — a dear

companion, lover, brother —
shivering. *Malignant.*

Outside
I'm swimming
through a hot storm
of light: head down
I hurry from shadow
to shadow, eyes on the ground,
where I see the fresh tar
sealing the driveway
is already cracked open with
little craters, irresistible shoots
of dandelion and crabgrass
knuckling up. Nothing can stop
their coming to a green point, this
hungry thrust towards light. Here

are seeds the songbirds will forage
as the weather hardens
before snow, green wounds
gleaming in tar, life itself
swallowing sunlight. The blacktop
glares at a clear blue sky
and in my eyes the sun
spins a dance of scalpels:
I pray for cloud, for
night's benign and cooling
graces, to be at ease again
in the friendly
city of shadows.

Walking Home As the Rain Draws Off

Bright pools of crowded light
I step across, odd drops
making the lot of it shiver,
giving each radiant
diminished world the shakes.

Crossing the borders of astonishment
a coppergreen roof after heavy rain
starts out of mist and flickering spume
and the eye sings in fright, is full
of weird joy, as if suddenly you heard
Vivaldi rising over broken houses,
the bombed city being dreamed
whole again, a swollen slope of
mineral green, light hatching on it.

Spirit weather, wreaths of mist
rising off the graveyard, the grey stones
gleaming to life again: nearby
I hear the dance instructor
shouting behind an open window
One and Two and One and Two and . . .
brusque commands so in the end
they'll move, the dancers will,
as light as mist in air, and pause
up there like second nature.

In front of me a mushrooming
procession of umbrellas
through the wet air — ivory,
lilac, chartreuse, jet black,
and one
with a jungle of shining vines, flesh-
coloured leopards bound in flowers,
canopy for the dark head
that keeps itself in check, those
two scrupulous feet
picking their dodgy way
over puddles of indecision
that say
only the rain is real, the rest
a dream that leads me — half
open wings, half stone — home.

At the end of the path
the bare birch blazes
beside the white house —
a branching wonder
brimming with light
in the neutral state
between seasons, between rain
and shine — the tree's pure gesture
saying simply *tree, light, tree,*
and I hear the birds call out
the dazzling passage
of rain, and the metal fence
I must pass through
is glazed at abrupt intervals
where the wet light strikes it.

Room and Sun

for my friends at MacDowell

When the sun comes directly in this window
I see nothing
but dazzle, molecular jazz
that splits the dancing atoms, breaking
the screen, the glass, the wooden frame
down to their original elements
in a flare-up of flashy gas. The big tree
outside — almost invisible
in this pelting and dismembering
brightness, as if its confident solidity
were nothing but a shortlived
trick of the light — brings to mind
John Donne
trying to stare his Maker down
and being sandblasted blind by light,
his fort of shreds and patches turning
to cinders in a wink, so absolute that
famished, unflinching look of love. But

when the sun sails to the side of the house
a whole world comes
alive and mobile and discrete
by its crooked light: little green shiverings
of leaf; pine needles in their peaceful rust;
touched-up tips of hemlock; pages and pages
of scattered brightness on the table
where a fern frond gathers bubbles of light
in water, and a white mug holds

my bent reflection. This oblique illumination
lets things be their limited
worldly selves: the silent
surface of a desk; the waiting patience
worn by two blue sheets; the black stem
balancing a desk lamp; my own
right hand's twigged shadow
sprouting across
this scribbled page.

Circlings

for Rachel & Kira

The full-bellied dress you move in
is a sail of light purple
to match the purple flowers
you've planted on the porch:
morning glories.
When it rains
I smell your patch of basil
in the back garden: come mid-winter
you'll draw pesto from the freezer
and give me again this dark
green fragrance, this
one touch of summer.

The little electric hum of her nerves
under my hand; her lungs
humming our latest air. The garden
a bed of dead leaves
where a young bird is born again
out of the cat's soft jaws. Milkblue,
the two eyes shine in her head.

Singing her hundred words for milk
she takes our noiseworld in. But what
in the marvelling moment's span of her attention
can she make of the frost feathers
glinting in the bedroom window
or the single fish-eye of light, olive-yellow,
swimming in oil in the slim bottle
after her bath? My face floats
down — a spiked cloud
of flesh and freckles, a sphere
of hairy thunder; my hand
a sea anemone
in a pool of air, my crook'd finger
a shy beast
brushing something
she can feel she feels.

In the corner under a nightlight
you sit in the rocking-chair
feeding the baby. From my pillow
I see the shadow-shapes
you two knit together,
how the line of your neck and throat
vanishes into the sweep of your hair
shawling the small
bald crown of her head
that's pressed against one
full breast. Your hands
catch light, moulding the globe of shadow
her head composes, steadying
that wool-bundled body

to your flesh. Wherever I look
in this world of light and shade,
the two of you are touching
one another, leaving me
exiled, not unhappy. And I'm asleep
and she's asleep
before you stretch
your warm length again beside me.

When the sun
glares in the window
and I leave our bed, the baby
is lying beside you, a half
smile on the lips
round your nipple: her eyes
are closed, your eyes are
closed, your head lightly resting
on top of hers. Downstairs
the geraniums and pink impatiens
press flushed winter faces
to the dining-room window
and everywhere
circles are slowly spinning
in circles, shadows dancing
through rings and widening rings of light.

In the kitchen you are ivory
cloves of garlic, the dark
green scalloped leaves
of romaine lettuce, one livid
drop of lemon on the tongue.
In the bed we wake and
very quietly make love
while the baby sleeps
on your other side: I can hear
in the world outside
the joyous contralto barking
of geese going over, going
south, widespread
across the sky — like a slung rosary.

Uphill Home

Two old men under the blazing
branches of late October go
slowly uphill home ahead of me.

I see, though they are dying, things
beginning to glow from inside out, the woods
a rose window of western light

over the two who lean into
one another's talk, shuffle and sway a little,
as if our solid ground grew spongy

under them. Their four hands flutter
like lated butterflies, one of them
lighting from time to time

on an elbow, a shoulder, and staying there
the way painted Monarchs stop
in the sun and stand, stunned,

in pure silence — waiting
for something, tuned to hear
whatever it is, something

secret and still — making
light of themselves and the state
they are in. I go home

behind two old men, in the wake
of their voices. A squirrel
crosses the road before us,

a fledge of dead leaves
bristling from its mouth: nest-builder,
his nerves must all be twigging

the next season
at the fretted edges
of this mulched and aromatic air.

In the leafless persimmon tree
little incandescent flesh bulbs
are lit, and the air in my mouth

is ripe fruit near rotting. This morning
I saw the grizzled first scurf of frost
on the quilted leaves of sugar maple

and now I'm wading through
all that fallen light
on its way to dust

behind two old men
whose voices don't carry
this far. I see the way

things work: it is the silence
of lichen edging out
the life of the tree; it is

the secret service of frost
bringing those bones
to light in the end; it is

the talking hands of the two old men
homing ahead of me. They
touch and flutter, touch again.

Breaking Points

for Joe Butwin

They all want to break at some point,
if you can only find it, he says, hoisting
the wedgeheaded heavy axe and coming down with it
in one swift glittering arc: a single *chunk*,
then the gleam of two half moons of maple
rolling over in the driveway. He finds
his proper rhythm, my strong friend from the west,
standing each half straight up,
then levelling swinging striking
dead centre: two quarters
fall apart from one another
and lie, off-white flesh shining,
on the cracked tarmac. I stand back
and watch him bend and bring to the chopping-place
a solid sawn-off wheel of the maple bough
the unexpected early snow brought down
in a clamorous rush of stricken leafage, a great weight
he walks gingerly under
and gently sets down. When he tests it with his eye

I remember a builder of drystone walls
saying the same thing about rocks and big stones,
turning one over and over, hunting its line
of least resistance, then offering it a little
dull tap with his mallet: the stone, as if he'd
slipped the knot holding it together, opened
— cloned — and showed its bright

inner life to the world. Joe goes on logging
for a furious hour, laying around him
the split quarters, littering the tar-black driveway
with their matte vanilla glitter. Seeing him
lean on the axe-shaft
for a minute's headbent silence
in the thick of his handiwork,

I remember standing in silence at the centre
of the living-room I was leaving for the last time
after ten years of marriage, the polished pine floor
scattered with the bits and pieces
I was taking with me,
the last battle still singing
in my head, the crossed limbs of the children
sofa-sprawled in sleep. And as soon as he finishes
and comes in, steam
sprouting from his red wet neck
and matted hair, dark maps of sweat
staining his navy blue T-shirt, I want to say
as he drains his second glass of lemonade

that this is the way it is
in the world we make and break
for ourselves: first the long green growing, then
the storm, the heavy axe, those shining remnants
that'll season for a year
before the fire gets them; this is the way
it is, this violent concentrated action
asserting ourselves to ourselves, the way we stand
and flail our way to freedom of a sort,
and after the heat and blistering deed of it
how the heart beats in its birdcage of bone

and you're alone
with your own staggered, sufficient body, its
toll taken, on the nervous verge
of exaltation. But I say nothing, pour more
lemonade, open a beer, listen to the tale he tells

of breakage back home — the rending-place
we reach when the labouring heart
fails us and we say, *What
now? What else? What?* In the dusk
assembling against the window,
I can see the big gouged maple
radiant where the bough stormed off,
and the split logs
scattered and bright over the driveway — in what
from this Babylonian distance looks like
a pattern of solid purposes or the end of joy.

Report from the Front

Roused from that sweet domestic sleep
I find no refuge, going in circles.

Leave the small house in its nest
of fuchsia, its garland of meadowsweet
and yellow rattle, go downhill
past the wooden ladder
listing against a grey unfinished gable, past
the raw glimmer of Atlantic blue — a platter
of cracked light. In the shimmering distance
the green heap of Mweelrea.

Covering old ground, all the ash trees bend
one way, scalded by salt and scorched
before their time by summer storms.

I sense a phantom limb, a sting
of weather, a veiled figure
stitched into dreams and
ticking over
in the empty phone-box, her face

averted. I know nothing
but a faint bodiless singing
or a sort of high talk I cannot catch
when the crazy door bangs
on broken hinges.

Driving through Fog

Who are these
acrobats of indiscretion,
her palm folded, flushed,
and smouldering in his?
Whose pulse ticking
the murder of clocks?

He knows her night-sky
and submarine blues, elusive
densities, whispers of bone.

Out of the fog's white throat
come crows, a mass of black
muscle, meandering cries. Blindly

he drives through a tunnel of steam,
declaring himself
at the border
of two weathers. Fireghosts whiten
off a shoulder of snow, bringing
green blades and bones to
milky light. Waves of light
breaking

where he finds himself
in the clear again, her face blazing
up from underground:
at this speed
he cannot turn.

Family Sketches

Forty years from the living-room window
I can see the children we were
ghosting among the apple trees, playing
hide-and-go-seek with my mother
among the bushes, holding our breath
against shadows. She'd cry out,
running in our direction
where we shivered with pleasure
at the sight of her in flight like that
over the grass — tilted forward and laughing,
her bare arms thrown wide open
to take us all in.

On the cracked footpath
outside what was once my grandmother's house
lies a crumpled sheet of last week's newspaper
smeared with blood and a black scab of flies
that batten, buzzing, on a clotted something
the colour of candlewax and
bleached kidney. As a child
I knew death twice
near this spot: my grandfather held my hand
in the Gypsies' Lane when we looked
down at Grex, his black dog,
and the emerald wings flickering
over his eyes and broken back; then
I am seeing my father

coming down the dark stairs
to tell us, *Grandad's gone to heaven*,
and the whole house smelling of stew,
snuff, heavy velvet, spent candles.

Pushing my mother in the borrowed wheelchair
among the cages at the Zoo
we stop under the mild eyes
of the giraffes. In her stroller
our daughter claps hands at that family
of slow-motion creatures
whose every bend
is a problem in physics. My mother
smiles, stares up at
the fantastic limbs and jungle colours
of that father, mother, and child
tall as trees in their grassy compound,
a tidy family thrown in
on itself, their great useless muscles intact
and, like a painful memory,
smouldering.

Driving west, a grey wall of cloud
slowly goes to bits ahead of me. This
is almost as far back as I remember.
A dark cloud, bright at its scalloped edges,
is breaking into rain or shine,
taking me away with my father

to small towns
at summer dusk, where for the first time
I met the friendly frightening smells
of porter and sawdust, whiskey,
plug tobacco, boiled cabbage,
and the cold scent of a strange room
for the two of us,
and the voices, laughter, clink of glasses
rising to where I lie alone and
wide-eyed in the night.

Kitchen Vision

Here in the kitchen, making breakfast,
I find my own view of things
come to light at last: I loom, huge
freckled hands, in the electric
kettle's aluminum belly. In there

the limegreen fridge, military files
of spice jars, and that transfigured window
where the sun breaks flagrant in,
must all recede, draw off, and join
the tiny mourning face
of Botticelli's Venus, hung
above a Lilliputian door. In there

our household effects
are strictly diminished, pared down
to brilliant miniatures
of themselves — the daily
ineluctable clutter of our lives
contained, clarified, fixed in place
and luminous in ordinary light
as if seen once and for all
by Jan Steen or Vermeer. And off

in the silver distance the baby
stares at me from her high chair
of a minute's silence,
and you — a mile away at the stove
turning the eggs — turn round

to look at me gazing
at my own
sharply seen misshapen self
in the kettle
that's just starting to sing,
its hot breath steaming.

Early Learning

Shackled to its blackness
and seeing it for the first time, she starts
babbling to the shape
of her own shadow
splashed on the dining-room's morning wall.

She sees it will do what she wants it to,
following and stopping, rising
and falling. She laughs
at her wriggling hand — a leaf, a dark
starfish — and wobbles her head

so the scalloped black circle on the wall
will wobble. She's beginning
to belong to herself, finding her own light
and shade sufficient. Draped
in a weightless cape of brightness,

she stands reading the darker side
of herself to herself
in silence: around the raggedy
shadow of her head
a sudden lightning play of wings, shadows

cast by the starlings
at the garden feeder: she startles, stares,
swivels to look for
the real birds over her shoulder,
snapping her two eyes shut

when the full light blinds her.

Compass Reading

The solid weights and shapes of anchors
inhabit every room. Chrysanthemum stems
in the Naples-yellow, womb-shaped vase
stand stiff as bars I look through
to the turning weather, the rose-of-Sharon bush
bent under the weight
of papery pink blossoms
bitten by a first frost, the birds
whose hungers sharpen, startling
their seasoned hearts
out of the leaves to our feeder
as the leaves give up their golden ghosts
and stiffen, dropping from branch to branch
with a small dry crash, paving the garden
and the road's margin
with, for a little while,
brightness.
          This morning
the cat pawed up against
the glass storm door, her eyes
wild and satisfied, a quiver
of pale grey-brown feathers
between her jaws. Shouting,
slamming open the door, I rescued
the broken neck, closed eyes, the tuft,
the ruffled wings — the chest
still soft and warm — and placed them
out of harm's way, as if it mattered,
in the mailbox. Later, under cover of the dark,
I took and threw the titmouse

among the leaves still clinging to trees and hedges
at the back of the house: flying
from my hand, I thought it gave
the smallest sigh, the way it
broke the air, the air
opening for it, taking its little weight
for the last time. I heard its faint, desiccated
splash among twigs and leaves
where it will lie, grow less itself, unravel
back to bone, to mould, to dust,
to next year's fierce leaf
whose feathers and fine airs
will stand up to anything. I imagine
its first arrested screech, the cat
tasting a salt smear of blood
across tongue and teeth: she knows
the ripe smell of death, the face
of terror, the terminal spasm.
                              These days
I seem as heartless as a lock
that is all innards and bitter tongue:
wherever my ears go
they hear nothing but clocks ticking, each tick
a distinct penetration of air, a pulsebeat
greeting its own goodbye. In the shortlived
gauze of dew on the front steps
I see the neat dark footpads
of the cat. And she will not
— for all her satisfactions —
be appeased.

Moving

She is moving
out over thresholds
of worn brass, under
scratched lintels.

The bones of the house
are showing, and all
its pitted edges, its
years of abiding.

The rain stops, leaving
behind it the slaphappy song
of full gutters, hornbeam
and hickory leaves

slick with light. She's been years
breathing and sleepwalking
among them, putting meals
on the shaky table, making

beds and other decisions.
She stands in the doorway
drinking the sky in, drowning
under a rush

of lilacs, drawn into
the frenzy of gnats
that riddle a patch of sunlight.
One eye on the baby

— whose hair floats
in its own silken haze — she will
hide herself at noon
in the shadows that travel

a sheet of unbleached cotton
caught between branches
and swaying in the sun. Folds
of shadow swell

and shrink: a mouth
of painted air, a world of shades
spilling out of it. Beautiful
and arching the arms

of branches. She is putting
it all behind her, wondering
what shape forgiveness
takes, what name

her father wore
in his suit of bamboo green, twirling
his whiskers for the ladies
and crooning ragtime, crooning

Schubert. Her mother's face
buries itself in the dust
behind the furniture,
turning away and saying

I told you so.
In the cellar
her husband the woodchuck
mopes among the spent

motors, rooting around
for her tongue. Nothing here
is home anymore,
from gilded doorknobs

to the timber
groaning at the heart
of plaster walls,
so she's moving out

into sea-light
that seems to run on
and on. When she's gone
she knows the dreams

will gather near the fireplace
like the smell of pine resin —
a faint perturbation
shaking the air. She knows

they will talk together
like elders, in low, slow,
fathoming voices, and then
set out to find her.

Station

We are saying goodbye
on the platform. In silence
the huge train waits, crowding the station
with aftermath and longing
and all we've never said
to one another. He
shoulders his black bag and shifts
from foot to foot, restless to be off, his eyes
wandering over tinted windows where he'll sit
staring out at the Hudson's platinum dazzle.

I want to tell him he's entering into the light
of the world, but it feels like a long tunnel
as he leaves one home, one parent
for another,
and we both know it won't ever
be the same again. What is the air at,
heaping between us, then thinning
to nothing? Or those slategrey birds that
croon to themselves in an iron angle, then
take flight, inscribing
huge loops of effortless grace
between this station of shade and the shining water?

When our cheeks rest glancing against each other,
I can feel mine scratchy with beard and stubble, his
not quite smooth as a girl's, harder, a faint fuzz
starting — those silken beginnings I can see
when the light is right, his next life
in bright first touches. What ails our hearts? Mine

aching in vain for the words
to make sense of our life together, his
fluttering in dread
of my finding the words, feathered syllables
fidgeting in his throat.

In a sudden rush of bodies
and announcements out of the air, he says
he's got to be going. One quick touch
and he's gone. In a minute
the train — ghostly faces behind smoked glass —
groans away on wheels and shackles, a slow glide
I walk beside, waving
at what I can see no longer. Later,
on his own in the city, he'll enter the underground
and cross the river, going home
to his mother's house: I imagine that white face
carried along in the dark glass, shining
through shadows that fill the window
and fall away again
before we're even able to name them.

Walk, Night Falling, Memory of My Father

Downhill into town
between the flaring azaleas
of neighbour gardens: a cairn of fresh-cut logs
gives off a glow
of broken but transfigured flesh.

My father meeting me years ago
off a train at Kingsbridge: greenish
tweed cap, tan gaberdine, leaning
on a rolled umbrella, the sun
in his eyes, the brown planes of his face
in shadow, and all of a sudden
old. The distance between us
closes to an awkward, stumbling
short embrace. Little left

but bits and pieces: pints in Healy's
before tea; a drive with visitors
to the Sally Gap; my daughter making
game with his glasses; the transatlantic calls
for an anniversary, birthday,
or to the hospital
before his operations. Moments
during those last days
in the ward, under the big window
where the clouds over the golf course
would break or darken: his unexpected
rise to high spirits, my hand

helping his hand
hold the glass of water. And one memory
he kept coming back to:
being a child in a white frock
watching his mother and another woman
in long white dresses and broad straw hats
recline in a rowing-boat on the Boyne
near Navan; how the boat rocked
side to side, the women smiling and
talking in low voices, and him
sitting by himself on the bank
in a pool of sunshine, his little feet
barely reaching the cool water. I remember
how the nurses swaddled his
thin legs in elastic bandages, keeping him
together for a day or two.

Uphill again, the dark now down
and the night voices
at their prayers and panicky conjurations,
one thrush bravely shaping
the air around him. Fireflies
wink on and off
in lovers' morse, my own head
floating among them, seeing
as each opens its heart in silence
and in silence closes
just how large the dark is. And now
new moonlight casts across this
shaking summer world a thin
translucent skin of snow; on ghostly wings
white moths brush by. Indoors again,
I watch them — fallen angels the size

and shade of communion wafers — beat
dusted wings against the screen, flinging
themselves at this impossible light.

THINGS
IN THE
FLESH

The Cave Painters

Holding only a handful of rushlight
they pressed deeper into the dark, at a crouch
until the great rock chamber
flowered around them and they stood
in an enormous womb
of flickering light and darklight, a place
to make a start. Raised hands cast flapping shadows
over the sleeker shapes of radiance.

They've left the world of weather and panic
behind them and gone on in, drawing the dark
in their wake, pushing as one pulse
to the core of stone. The pigments mixed in big shells
are crushed ore, petals and pollens, berries
and the binding juices oozed
out of chosen bark. The beasts

begin to take shape from hands
and feather-tufts (soaked in ochre, manganese,
madder, mallow white) stroking
the live rock,
letting slopes and contours mould
those forms from chance, coaxing
rigid dips and folds and bulges
to lend themselves to necks, bellies, swelling
haunches, a forehead or a twist of horn,
tails and manes curling to a crazy gallop.

Intent and human, they attach
the mineral, vegetable, animal

realms to themselves, inscribing the one unbroken line
everything depends on, from that impenetrable centre
to the outer intangibles of light and air, even
the speed of the horse, the bison's fear, the gentle arch
that big-bellied cow throws over
its spindling calf, or the lancing dance of death
that bristles out of the struck buck's
flank. In this one line they place
a beak-headed human figure of sticks
and one small, chalky, amputated hand.

We'll never know if they worked in silence
like people praying — the way our monks
illuminated their own dark ages
in rocky cloisters where the waves kept time
against invasions and the weather,
as they contrived a binding labyrinth
of laced and fabulous lit affinities
to spell their blinding sixth sense out
of a god of shadows — or whether,
like birds tracing their own great bloodlines
over the globe, they kept a constant gossip up
of praise, encouragement, complaint.

It doesn't matter. We know
they went with guttering rushlight
into the dark; came to terms
with the given world; must have had
— as their hands moved steadily
by spiderlight — one desire
we'd recognise: they would, before going on
beyond this border zone, this nowhere
that is now here, leave something
upright and bright behind them in the dark.

Endangered Species

Out the living-room window
I see the two older children burning
household trash under the ash tree
in wind and rain. They move
in slow motion about the flames,
heads bowed in concentration
as they feed each fresh piece in, hair
blown wild across their faces, the fire
wavering in tongues before them
so they seem creatures
half flame, half flesh,
wholly separate from me. All of a sudden

the baby breaks slowly down
through the flexed branches of the ash
in a blaze of blood and green leaves, an
amniotic drench, a gleaming liver-purple
slop of ripe placenta, head first
and wailing to be amongst us. Boy and girl
look up in silence and hold gravely out
flamefeathered arms to catch her,
who lands on her back in their linked
and ashen hands. Later, when I take her in my arms

for a walk to that turn in the high road
where the sea always startles, I can see
how at intervals she's thunderstruck
by a scalloped green leaf, a shivering
jig of grassheads, or the speckled bee

who pushes himself among
the purple and scarlet parts
of a fuchsia bell. And her eyes are on fire.

Small Mercies

From where I stand I can see the chipmunk
scrabbling at dead leaves, the blonde girl
reaching to touch, just kissed, her boy's
tilted face, the labouring geese going over
with the south in grain, sparing no
migrant eye for the squashed rabbit, the fox's
broken neck, the wounded deer waiting for snow.

Light brings the baby back, her moonstruck
moans and drowsy humming. The groundhog
fattens into winter, and the lost boy
comes groping to show me again at sunset
on Menemsha Bay how he bends, picks, leans
a little to one side and skips a stone over
blazing water: it dances, dripping fire, hissing
and clicking, sinking into a huge silence.

Here at home gruel-coloured sunlight
smears the metal fence, a line of laundry
shines like four November ghosts
hanging out where the neighbours' cats
kill the springy wind-quick
fallen leaves. When darkness seeps
around the house, I stand on the steps
and see through the lit window mother and child
smile at one another, and for a moment
there's a risk that joy will
show my bones up. In plain daylight

I see the winter leaf would fall
as the plummet falls
if the bracing air didn't drive it
to distraction, to an afterlife
of plunges and reluctance, second
thoughts and hesitations
all the way down. I'm trying
to find a place for the beautiful
evasions of the body: the way

that purple finch, for example, dodges
in open acres of air the falcon's
right hook and talon; or how the crow
shrugs his bones and shakes his feathers
so a jetblack back flashes
and flings off small throbbing splashes
of light. I've seen it all
before, not knowing
what I was seeing: a world of forms
bursting into flames in front of me, sudden espousals
of air and solid matter. And it is there too

in the wavering tall walls of mist
rising off snow in a sudden thaw, the cold
heart of things being taken by surprise: this
is the beginning of bodies and their end —
the way, in spite of solid flesh, we would
dissolve in one another. And is at last
a lonesome gathering of ghosts
in the open: like a dumbfounded
family of refugees they hover
around and around one another, turning and
touching and whispering before they go.

Woman at Lit Window

Perhaps if she stood for an hour like that
and I could stand to stand in the dark
just looking, I might get it right, every
fine line in place: the veins of the hand
reaching up to the blind-cord, etch
of the neck in profile, the white
and violet shell of the ear
in its whorl of light, that neatly
circled strain against a black
cotton sweater. For a few seconds

she is staring through me
where I stand wondering what I'll do
if she starts
on that stage of light
taking her clothes off. But she only
frowns out at nothing or herself
in the glass, and I think I could,
if we stood for an hour like this,
get some of the real details down. But
already, even as she lowers the blind,
she's turning away, leaving a blank

ivory square of brightness
to float alone in the dark, the faint
grey outline of the house
around it. Newly risen, the half moon casts
my shadow on the path
skinned with grainy radiance

as I make my way back
to my own place
among the trees, a host of fireflies
in fragrant silence and native ease
pricking the dark around me
with their pulse of light.

Breakfast Room

1

The words have always stirred a sudden
surge of light, an air of new beginnings, something
neat and simple, a space
both elemental and domestic — because, perhaps,
they bear a sort of innocent sheen
of privilege, a room so set apart
for an event so ordinary, a glimmer of ritual
where mostly we know only broken facts, bits and pieces
stumbling numbly into one another. Here
is a murmur of voices, discretion's homely music
of spoons on saucers, the decent movements
people make around each other — eager
to let themselves become themselves again
after the uncertain journeys of the night. Or it may be
the secret knowing smiles that lovers save, sitting
to face one another in their quaint conspiracy
of hope and saying, *Pass the milk, please*, but meaning
Nothing has ever pleased me more
than how your naked shoulders and the small of your back
lay on my spread hands; your earlobe, tongue, wide eyes
entering half-frightened mine in the dark.

2

And in Bonnard's *The Breakfast Room* you'll see
the impeccable ordinary order he finds in things: white,
slateblue, the tablecloth bears its own still life

of teapot, cream pitcher, sugarbowl, china cup
and scalloped saucer, the half glass of raspberry juice,
bread in yellow napkins, that heaped dish
of purple figs and a peach. And, as if
accidental by the French windows —
through which morning light
passes its binding declarative sentence
on every detail — a woman stands
almost out of the picture, her back
against the patterned drapes, dressed to go out
and giving a last look back, her eyes and strict lips
asking directly, *You think this
changes anything?* Yet she too
is part of this stillness, this sense that things
are about to achieve
illumination. Beyond the window
a stone balustrade, and beyond that
nature's bluegreen tangle tangles
with the light that's melting one thing
into another — blue, scrubbed green, strawgold,
a house with a white and lilac roof
at the dead end of a sunstreaked avenue
on which the trees are
blobs of turquoise. Inside and quite distinct, that woman
is held to her last look back, her
sudden pulsebeat shaking
all the orderly arrangements
of the table. Through its ambivalence of light,
its double tongue of detail and the world at large,
we are brought into the picture, into a kingdom
we might find under our noses: morning's
nourishment and necessary peace; a pause
on the brink of something always
edging into shape, about to happen.

Branchwater

Full Sail

The city spread its blue room of toys
at our feet, firebushes
burning a sinister crimson, the sea
a bluegrey tablecloth
in the damask distance. Warm hair.
The ridge of your throat.

The train I leave on
winds round coastline hemmed with surf:
blue and yellow flowers
open-mouthed
in the parched gardens.

Walking away down the platform
you turned with a question,
but I'd said nothing
and you kept on going, stepping
against the rush-hour crowd.

When we sat next to the water
the boats almost came over us:
tall masts at a windy tilt, bright sails
taut round their bodies of air.
Butterflies, they skim the very
brink of water, courting disaster.

Flowering Branch

You'd sail full tilt into my mornings,
your bloodred shopping-bag
banging against you, thronging the air
with your tonguetied family of shadows.

Once you stood in front of me
gripping a yellow branch — forsythia —
and were for a minute the pure spirit
of that casual place, flowering

and broken. The swelling light
held you like an old flame
in perfect silence, both of us
with nothing to say. Then,

flailing at whatever it was that
discomposed you, you stepped
intrepidly away from me
into those early shadows, leaving

me the dear spate of your voice
dashing off secrets and
scabrous stories; those glib splinters of light
pointing each yellow petal; this

Dead Sea thirst; a clean pair of heels.

Woman Holding a Balance

— Vermeer

Almost invisible, a minute affair
of metal, she holds it dead steady
between a thumb and one finger.

Crossbar, arms and pans: in the picture
each one's an arsenic-white line
no thicker than a squirrel's hair,

but her attention on them
absolute, a gravity so specific
she might be pondering her whole life

in this chosen moment. She pays no notice
to the cascade-embrace
of light he's laid upon her

from the gold-scarfed crown of her head
down the winter-ermine borders of fur
that keep her breasts in check, a light

unleashed and obsessive, an inquisition
of eager daylight that — entering
by a high window — illuminates

one shoulder, barely, and the bone
of her throat. Half her left arm
glows, down-stippled, in it,

while the fingernails and knuckles
of her right hand are touched
so deftly and irrevocably that

their flesh and tiny nacred ovals
will carry the sign of his eyes forever
or as long as oil and egg-white

last. She stands with one hand
on the table, not really leaning,
as if her weight were all gone

to her invisible heart, the rest
scarcely registering as a fact, a
heavy fact of matter. This

kiss of light from brow to
distended belly — where burnt crimson
briefly flashes — has taken her

over, weighing her daily elements,
placing them precisely
in the scale of things. Behind her

a darkened square of canvas: Christ
in a small lunette
of clouded light, arms raised

over a day of judgement, the naked
bodies of the damned or saved
in a pale throng waiting

at the bottom, stripped to their last
gasp of value. Standing
back from the picture

I see the real balance
is the one the painter struck
between the throbbing light

that finds her there — alive
and a little off centre — and those
opposing zones of dark:

that last darkness
where the soul rides
a final time at anchor

in the baffled body;
and a lush underwater
dark of cinnabar

that brims from the folds of heavy cloth
bundled out to
the table's far corner, a mass

of secular depths and
coaxing angles, a material
void. Revealed,

the bare board of the table
is spread with oaklight, sprinkled
with pearls, smeared with

coils of gold, and on it
the bright, fleshed fingers
of her left hand — slightly

flexed — depend.

Cows

They lay great heads on the green bank
and gently nudge the barbed wire aside
to get at the sweet untrodden grass, ears
at an angle flicking and swivelling.
Something Roman in the curled brow, massive
bony scaffolding of the forehead,
the patient, wary look that's
concentrated but detached, as if
the limits of being didn't matter
behind such a lumbering surge of things
in the flesh. Yet in their eyes
some deep unspeakable secret grudge — in part
a perfect knowledge of
the weight of the world
we hold them to. And something Dutch
about that recumbent mass, their couchant
hefty press of rumination, the solid globe
folded round the ribs' curved hull,
barrelling that enormous belly. The close
rich smell of them
grinding down grass to milk
to mother us all, or the childhood smell of stalls
all milk and piss and dungy straw:
what that umbered word, *cowshed*, conjures.

I remember an Indian file of cows in mist
moving along the lake's lapped margin,
a black and white frieze
against the green hill that
leaned over them: the sound

of their cloven steps in shallow water
reached me like the beat of a settled music
in the world we share; and they could have been
plodding towards Lascaux or
across broad prairie-seas of green, even
trampling water-edges
such as this one, trudging through the kingdom-come
of sagas and cattle-raids. Heads bent,
they stepped into mist and silence, the pooling
splash of their hooves a steady progress
that seemed to go on forever, forged
for an eternal trek to grass.

I love the way a torn tuft
of grassblades, stringy buttercup and succulent clover
sway-dangles towards a cow's mouth, the mild teeth
taking it in — purple flowers, green stems and yellow petals
lingering on those hinged lips
foamed with spittle. And the slow chewing sound
as transformation starts: the pulping roughness
of it, its calm deliberate solicitude, its
entranced herbivorous pacific
grace, the carpet-sweeping sound of breath
huffing out of pink nostrils. Their eyelashes
— black, brown, beige, or white as chalk —
have a minuscule precision, and in the pathos
of their diminutive necessity
are the most oddly human thing about them: involuntary,
they open, close,
dealing as our own do
with what inhabits, encumbering,
the seething waves and quick invisible wilderness
of air, showing the one world
we breathe in

and the common ground — unsteady
under the big whimsical hum
of weather — we all walk across
one step at a time, and stand on.

Daughter and Dying Fish

Cast out on this stone pier, the dogfish are dying
in a simmering sunlit heap of torcs
and contortions, bristlemouths propped open

in a silent scream against
the treacherous element of air, a yawn
of pure despair, the soft slap of fantails

sliding the slow length of one another
as spines stiffen, scales shimmer, glaucous
sea-eyes pop with shock and resignation

when my cloudy shadow trawls across them.
She stands balancing her twenty months
on twisted arm-thick hanks of rope

and is no more than a moment perplexed
when she bends to touch a spine, those
fading scales, and then goes back

to the song she was singing, turning
from what I can't take my eyes off:
their cloudy eyes, the slow weave

of their singular limbs, slubbered
smack of oily skin on skin, the faint heaving motion
of the whole mass like one body

beating away from the face of the earth.
How they would glide, barely brushing
one another, bodies all curve and urgency

in their glimmering space
and humming chambers, their swift unravellings
of desire or death, who now lie

in the raw elusive air and wait
for what comes next, a hapless
heap of undulant muscle, a faint, fierce

throbbing. Gently the sea
slaps at these stone foundations
laid to stand the winter storms

without shaking: smooth as skin,
the granite surfaces gleam
like live things in sunlight

where my daughter walks,
a cheerful small voice
still singing.

Sea Dog

The sea has scrubbed him clean
as a deal table. Picked over, plucked
hairless, drawn tight as a drum,
an envelope of tallow
jutting with rib cage, hips,
assorted bones. The once
precise pads of his feet are
buttons of bleached wood
in a ring of stubble. The skull —
bonnetted, gap-toothed, tapering
trimly to a caul of wrinkles —
wears an air faintly
human, almost ancestral.

Now the tide falls back
in whispers, leaving the two of us
alone a moment together. Trying to take in
what I see, I see the lye-bright
parchment skin scabbed black
by a rack of flies
that rise up, a humming chorus,
at my approach, settle again when I
stop to stare. These must be
the finishing touch, I think,
until I see round the naked neckbone
a tightly knotted
twist of rope, a frayed noose
that hung him up or held him under
until the snapping and jerking stopped.

Such a neat knot: someone knelt
safely down to do it, pushing those ears back
with familiar fingers. The drag end
now a seaweed tangle around legs
stretched against their last leash.

And nothing more
to this sad sack
of bones, these poor enduring remains
in their own body bag. Nothing more.
Death's head here
holds its own peace
beyond the racket-world of feel and fragrance
where the live dog bent, throbbing
with habit, and the quick children
now shriek by on sand — staring,
averting. I go in over my head

in stillness, and see
behind the body and the barefoot children
how on the bent horizon to the west
a sudden flowering shaft of sunlight
picks out four pale haycocks
saddled in sackcloth
and makes of them a flared quartet
of gospel horses — rearing up,
heading for us.

Rights

He has every right to name her.
The nimble muse of History
is what the poet said, rolling his Russian
consonants and vowels around at us
like gravel, *gravitas*, like gravity, the solid
slow motion towards the core. She's

been to bed with him, both of them
out in the cold and tonguetied, but oh,
the oily motions of her quickened limbs
there in the dark, nothing between them
but, thin as air, the knifeblade and
— thinner than that — the flash of it
where their blind hips touch,
knowing one another for what they are.

He has earned her name, living at home
for years with her like that, her
bruised lips on his, his eyes wide open
to every wrinkle, nick, and imperfection
of age in her, the blackened orbs
of her eyelids, her cracked hands. She is
never the same as he remembers her:

a voice from childhood or a flicker
of cobbled light off water; the door
knocked open at two in the morning
or a letter from a friend in exile; silence
on the very edge of revelation. Or else the raw

igniting ice then fire of vodka
tongued and swallowed; the heartfelt
smell of morning — fresh bread, blue spruce,
snow in May — all the feints, glides and
fancy handwork of that muse of his,

who is nimble as a dancer at the court
of amazement, her beautiful bleeding feet
barely tipping the double blade
she bows and balances and spins on.

One Morning during the Elections

In the washed lucidity of the hill
a barn's red roof is visible.
White houses clinging to green rock;
the silver glint of windows.

Switching off the radio,
I walk into the early morning
and the first sun for days. Birds
lift eager voices after the long storm
and one lark is out of his high mind
in a manic fling of gracenotes
and crazy modulations
until breath fails and he
falls, a feathered
stone, into a furze bush.

The drenched grass is white
under this light, where big-beamed
slow cows shift through
sudden sprays of brightness,
their mild jaws filling stillness
with a rich chomping. Ash leaves
hang almost idle, scarcely shivering
as the air around them
changes. The fuchsia's
brilliant ignitions
set the wet hedges on fire
under a small hawk that
glides across pastureland

towards the foam-fringed,
blue table of the lake.

The voices I walked out on
send their echoes after me.
Something unspeakable in the state:
a severed head, slow punctures
all over the heart; the hard facts
leaking through this natural thatch.

But here is the black button eye
of the speckled young robin
at the feeder, the maize-yellow
bill of the blackbird, grass
glittering after rain, that indifferent
singleminded glide of the hawk,
his one hunger. And in the distance

the whitewashed houses shine
like chosen things, like small
deceptive settlements
of peace; cloudshadows
cross the tranquil dazzle
of the bay, the air
brimming
with the sudden black hum
of hungry flies
that greet the seeping day;
Jacob's ladders
of inexpressible light run down
out of the clouds, stand
on the water, on the stony hills.

Colour Shot

Outside a South African shanty
a line of laundry shines
behind a boy's full, foregrounded face,
his eyes hidden in
enormous orange-rimmed sunglasses.

The washing's a cloud of
white sheets, an umber quilt, three
almond blouses and a fierce
vermillion shirt, all frozen
under a steel and sapphire sky.

The boy stares straight out. A dozen
rusty surfaces come lurching
into splintered light. And behind it all
the rising clear line of fresh washing
gleams in the breeze, a civil sign

and morning offering
to the belief that clean sheets
will mount, like clouds, the air
and swell there, that shirts
will be lathered, rinsed, jounced, wrung out,

then hung to dry and lighten
towards the skin they'll shine on.
In these household flags
of no surrender, these signs
of life that harkens after brightness,

you might find the hearth's
own crooked smoke
ascending, or find
some saving grace to flourish
in the open eye of heaven.

That Ocean

To love the scrubbed exactitudes
and the dimmer thing
that shivers at the brink.

There is, for example, the intimate rustle
of this woman's loose skirt, rayon,
as she hurries up a flight of stone steps
ahead of me: I slow down to relish
the faintly kissing sound of threads,
threads and flesh.

Or under a quilted bundling-up of cloud
a crow's broad black wing
palping air: dark assemblage
of force and voice and appetite and air,
a poise, a buoyancy, a beating
of bone light as breath, burning with purpose.

I despair of dealing sincerely
with the crow, the brushings of desire,
that woman's headlong motion, the black farewell,
steady caresses opening the air,
inflamed soliloquy of the skirt,
fragrant dialogue of flesh and texture.

Under this abrasive rain the grass,
dead all winter,
glows like straw-spun fabled gold
and two kinds of willow
— the local and the Babylonian —

flush and swell demented: one
rises in upright ecstasy, the other
overarched with grief. They
occupy the wary air
with embering green, bleached amber,
and when the rain grows less
I can hear the little singers
going mad again.

Or there is the absolute intimacy
of eating. To stand in the kitchen
sniffing a bowl of duck fat
is to catch a scent
the creature never had of itself: it is
offering up its essence
the way neck feathers offered once
an iridescence to the eye one morning
as it swivelled in front of you
on a flat dazzle of water. And so
our own essence
is by nature beyond us,
will be rendered after.

At uncommon intervals of attention
we remember ourselves
at one with this world: we enter
the network, a thicket of stillness
where in early spring a sapling of apple or cherry
sends out where it stands
inside the wire fence containing the graveyard
spray after spray of blossom
to stagger the eye
at the solid grey threshold
of tombstones scoured by rain . . . .

And this may be, you imagine, what
in the dream of good government
Lorenzetti's Peace is dreaming
where she lounges —
relaxed, empty, ready for anything
— for the end of art, is it, or
simply listening into
what might happen, the grasp
of dancers in a ring, their linked hands
a finished circle? Through it all, all
this seething, I walk
beneath a black umbrella, behind
a bright bead curtain of rain.

Leftovers

The silken limegreen wings of two luna moths
pulsing gently on the shadowed screen door
all morning. A stretch of thigh
bared in sunlight — silksmooth and tanned between
sandalwood and dry sherry. A faint
scarlet fleck along one cheekbone, white
twist of silk scarfing the throat. Mooncurve
of a brick-pink fingernail; tonguetip
vanishing behind a gleam of teeth or
travelling — all fleshed texture and blood-heat —
the nicked lip, making it glisten. A black smudge
thickening a single eyelash,
and under a light rose-checkered dress
the long outline
of a leg, a solid shadow. One hand
splayed on the breathing rise and fall
of a brown belly, like a painted hand
come to light on a cave wall
where torches streel and leap
across the dark. Or else
it is a calf-length skirt of early mist, a blouse
birchleaf green, one goldspiked
lavender glitter of garnets, a sandal's
spiralling leather strap, jangling brass anklets
or the sudden juddering ripple of a hip
as the breath stops and then comes
back again in time. Such abandoned
bits and pieces
my eyes have picked over

like seagulls living off scraps
the tide has left: in me they quicken, rising
as whole bodies again
and all their covered, incandescent bones.

Two Gathering

After supper, the sun sinking fast, Kate and I
have come to the shore at Derryinver
to gather mussels. Across cropped grass, rocks,
we walk to the water's edge where low tide
has exposed a cobbling of cobalt blue shells, others
tucked in clusters under a slick fringe
of seaweed. In my wellingtons
I enter shallow water, bending over
and wresting from their native perch
the muddy clumps of molluscs, rinsing them
in salt water that clouds and quickly clears again
as the tide laps, a slow cat, against me, then
pushing my handfuls into the white plastic bag
I've laid out of the water's way on seaweed.
Kate, in sneakers, is gathering hers
off the dry rocks behind me: almost sixteen,
her slim form blossoms in jeans
and a black T-shirt, long hair falling over
as she bends, tugs, straightens with
brimming hands, leans like a dancer
to her white bag, looks out to me and calls
So many! Have you ever seen so many! her voice
a sudden surprise in that wide silence
we stand in, rejoicing — as she always does
and now I must — at the breathless plenitude
of the world, this wondrous abundance
offering itself up to us as if we were masters
of the garden, parts of the plenary sphere
and circle, our bodies belonging
to the earth, the air, the water, fellow

creatures to the secret creatures we gather
and will tomorrow kill for our dinner.

When I bend again — my hands pale groping starfish
under water — it is Kate's own life I fumble for,
from the crickets singing her name
that September afternoon she was born
to the balance she strikes
between separated parents, her passion
for maths, the names of her lost boys,
or the way she takes my arm
when we take a walk on Wing Road
or up the hill from Tully to the cottage. This instant
I can feel her eyes on my bent back, seeing me
standing over my ankles in water, the slow
tide climbing my boots, my cautious
inelastic stepping between elements
when I place the mussels I've gathered
in the bag. And if I turn to look,
I'll see a young woman rising out of sea-rocks, bearing
the salmon and silver air on her shoulders,
her two hands spilling a darkblue arc, about
to take a dancer's step: I hear the muffled clack
of live shells filling her bag.

In our common sphere of silence we're aware
of one another, working together, until
she calls out — *Have you seen*
their colours? Brown and olive and bright green
and black. I thought they were only navy blue —
delighted by variety, the minute ripple of things
under water or changing in air, the quick patterns,
as if the world were one intricate vast equation
and she relished picking it over, seeing the figures

unfold and in a split surprising second
edge out of muddle into elegant sense, the way
she's explained to me her love of maths
as a journey through multiple views to a moment
of — yes, she said it — 'vision', you simply see it
all in place before your eyes: a flowering branch
of impeccable sense; number and grace
shimmering in a single figure; a shard of truth
shining like the head of a new nail
you've just, with one stroke, driven home.

Feeling the drag and push of water, I know it's time
to move and I do, inching backwards, my hands
still scrabbling under rubbery fronds of seaweed
for the mussels' oval stony bulk, their brief
umbilical resistance as I twist them
from their rock, swirl in water, add them
with drippling chill hands to the bag, sensing
the summer dusk falling all over us. *Dad, look! A heron!*
standing not twenty yards from us
on the hem of the tide: a grey stillness
staring at nothing
then flicking his serpent-neck and beak
into the water and out, taking a single deliberate step
and then on slow opening wings rising and
flap-gliding across the inlet, inland, heavy
and graceful on the air, his legs
like bright afterthoughts dangling. *He's so big,*
she calls, *How does he do it?* and across the raw
distance of rock and water I call back,
It's the span of his wings, he uses the air,
thinking about question and answer, the ways
we're responsible to one another, how we
use our airy words to lift us up

above the dragging elements we live in
towards an understanding eloquent and silent
as blood is or the allergies I've handed
to her system — our bodies' common repugnance
to penicillin, sulfa — all the buried codes
that bind us in a knot even time
cannot untangle, diminishing, in a way,
the distance between us. *Did you see,* I hear my voice,
his legs? The way they dangled? Thin — her voice
comes back to me — *as sticks, and the colour
of pearl. Funny the way he tucked them in,
putting them away,* and she drops a castanet
handful of mussels into her bag.
                                    My hands
are blueish, a small breeze riffles the water,
the spur of land we're on is drowned
in shade: we've gathered enough
and it's time to go. She watches me wading
through bright, light-saving pools, reaches
a helping hand when I clamber up rock
above the line of seaweed where she stands waiting
on grass the sheep have bitten to a scut,
their tidy shit-piles of black pellets
scattered all over. With pleasure we behold
the two bulging bags I've draped
in glistering layers of olivebrown bladderwrack,
both of us thinking of the dinner we'll have
tomorrow: brown bread, white wine, a green
salad, the steaming heaps of open shellfish
— ribboned in onion, carbuncled
with chunks of garlic — the plump dull-orange
crescent of each one gleaming
in its mottled shell, sea-fragrance curling off
the greybright salty peppered soup

they've offered up to us, and in it the brilliance
of lemon wedges swimming. At least once each summer
we have a family feast like this, and I picture
her delight in the dipping of buttered bread, laying
a hot mussel on her tongue, the squirt of sea-tang and flesh
against her teeth, sipping the wine that's still
a stranger to her palate, remembering
the way the sun went down behind the two of us
as we gathered dinner, as if our lives
were always together and this simple.
                                        Now
we stand side by side for a minute or two
in silence, taking the small bay in and the great shade
spreading over sea and land: across the water,
on a sloping headland of green fields, we see
how a stopped hand of sunlight still
in the middle distance lingers, brightening
one brief patch of ground with uncanny light
so I cannot tell if I'm looking at a moment past
of perfect knowledge, or a bright future
throbbing with promise. Then Kate
is giving me, again, her words: *I wonder
will it strike us over here*, is what
I hear her say — her words, unanswered,
hanging between us as we turn to go.

Notes

page 29   The line in italics was prompted by a phrase in the poem 'Bords' by Michel Deguy.

page 55   Bonnard's 'The Breakfast Room' is in the Museum of Modern Art, New York.

page 59   Vermeer's 'A Lady Weighing Gold' is in the National Gallery of Art, Washington, D.C.

page 68   Among the things in my head when I was writing 'Sea Dog' were the Bog Poems of Seamus Heaney.

page 70   The line in italics is Evgenii Rein's, heard in a reading he gave at Vassar College in 1989.

page 78   The figure of Peace appears in Ambrogio Lorenzetti's 'Allegory of Good and Bad Government' in the Palazzo Pubblico, Siena.

Acknowledgements

Acknowledgements are due to the editors of the following publications in which some of these poems first appeared: *Agni*, *Antaeus*, *Columbia Magazine*, *Thistledown*, *Éire-Ireland*, *Grand Street*, *The Kenyon Review*, *New England Review*, *The Ontario Review*, *Southwest Review*, *The Threepenny Review* and *Wigwag*.

The poems 'Breakfast Room', 'Compass Reading', 'Cows', 'Kitchen Vision', 'Report from the Front', 'Room and Sun', 'Sea Dog', 'Small Mercies', 'That Ocean', 'Two Climbing', 'Uphill Home' and 'Walk, Night Falling, Memory of My Father' appeared originally in the *New Yorker*.

'The Cave Painters' appeared originally in *Poetry*.

My warm thanks to Alice Quinn and Louis Asekoff. I would also like to thank Peter Fallon of The Gallery Press. I am grateful to the directors and staff of the MacDowell Colony for their enabling hospitality.

The biggest debt remains, to Rachel.

OTHER POETRY FROM GRAYWOLF

NINA BOGIN / *In the North*

ROSARIO CASTELLANOS / *The Selected Poems of Rosario Castellanos*, translated by Magda Bogin

JOHN ENGELS / *Cardinals in the Ice Age*

TESS GALLAGHER / *Amplitude: New and Selected Poems*
  Moon Crossing Bridge
  Under Stars

CHRISTOPHER GILBERT / *Across the Mutual Landscape*

JACK GILBERT / *Monolithos: Poems, 1962 & 1982*

DANA GIOIA / *Daily Horoscope*
  The Gods of Winter

LINDA GREGG / *Alma*
  Too Bright to See
  The Sacraments of Desire

RICHARD GROSSMAN / *The Animals*

EMILY HIESTAND / *Green, the Witch-Hazel Wood*

VICENTE HUIDOBRO / *Altazor*, translated by Eliot Weinberger

ROBERT JONES / *Wild Onion*

JANE KENYON / *The Boat of Quiet Hours*
  Let Evening Come

VALERIO MAGRELLI / *Nearsights: Selected Poems*, translated by Anthony Molino

EUGENIO MONTALE / *Mottetti: Poems of Love*, translated by Dana Gioia

JACK MYERS / *As Long as You're Happy*

A. POULIN, JR. / *Cave Dwellers*
  A Momentary Order

RAINER MARIA RILKE / *The Complete French Poems of Rainer Maria Rilke*, translated by A. Poulin, Jr.

JEFFREY SKINNER / *A Guide to Forgetting*

WILLIAM STAFFORD / *Smoke's Way*

JAMES L. WHITE / *The Salt Ecstasies*

Praise for

AS IF IT
MATTERS

"Eamon Grennan's poems are like late 20th century verbal equivalents of 17th century Dutch paintings. How luminously they capture the brimming fullness of daily life, how scrupulously they come to terms with the complex reality of the limited, given world, how radiantly they clarify 'the daily/ineluctable clutter of our lives.' These poems shine and matter." —EDWARD HIRSCH

"This new collection contains some of his [Eamon Grennan's] most telling work, and with so fine a poet that is saying a great deal." —W.S. MERWIN

"With a grace and precision such as come only with a perfect ear, Eamon Grennan welcomes us into the midst of that place where thoughts and sensations somehow magically come together and coexist as one. What he shows us there is now grave, now playful, but never less than life-enhancing." —AMY CLAMPITT